CHILDREN'S STORYTELLERS

# Gordon Korman

by Chris Bowman

BELLWETHER MEDIA • MINNEAPOLIS, MN

Note to Librarians, Teachers, and Parents:

**Blastoff! Readers** are carefully developed by literacy experts and combine standards-based content with developmentally appropriate text.

**Level 1** provides the most support through repetition of high-frequency words, light text, predictable sentence patterns, and strong visual support.

**Level 2** offers early readers a bit more challenge through varied simple sentences, increased text load, and less repetition of high-frequency words.

**Level 3** advances early-fluent readers toward fluency through increased text and concept load, less reliance on visuals, longer sentences, and more literary language.

**Level 4** builds reading stamina by providing more text per page, increased use of punctuation, greater variation in sentence patterns, and increasingly challenging vocabulary.

**Level 5** encourages children to move from "learning to read" to "reading to learn" by providing even more text, varied writing styles, and less familiar topics.

Whichever book is right for your reader, Blastoff! Readers are the perfect books to build confidence and encourage a love of reading that will last a lifetime!

This edition first published in 2018 by Bellwether Media, Inc.

No part of this publication may be reproduced in whole or in part without written permission of the publisher. For information regarding permission, write to Bellwether Media, Inc., Attention: Permissions Department, 5357 Penn Avenue South, Minneapolis, MN 55419.

Library of Congress Cataloging-in-Publication Data

Names: Bowman, Chris, 1990- author.
Title: Gordon Korman / by Chris Bowman.
Description: Minneapolis, MN : Bellwether Media, Inc., 2018. | Series: Blastoff! Readers: Children's Storytellers | Includes bibliographical references and index. | Audience: Grades 2-5
Identifiers: LCCN 2016055075 (print) | LCCN 2017013273 (ebook) | ISBN 9781626176485 (hardcover : alk. paper) | ISBN 9781681033785 (ebook)
Subjects: LCSH: Korman, Gordon–Juvenile literature. | Authors, American–20th century–Biography–Juvenile literature. | Children's stories–Authorship–Juvenile literature.
Classification: LCC PS3561.O3398 (ebook) | LCC PS3561.O3398 Z55 2018 (print) | DDC 813/.54 [B] –dc23
LC record available at https://lccn.loc.gov/2016055075

Editor: Betsy Rathburn          Designer: Josh Brink

Printed in the United States of America, North Mankato, MN.

# Table of Contents

# Who Is Gordon Korman?

Gordon Korman is a best-selling author of more than 80 books for children and teens. He is known for creating the Swindle and Masterminds **series**.

His stand-alone **novels** such as *Ungifted* and *Schooled* are also favorites for many. More than 28 million copies of Gordon's books have been sold around the world!

Gordon was born on October 23, 1963, in Montreal, Canada. He was an only child. For much of his childhood, his family lived near Toronto, Canada.

"I guess I knew writing was the career for me in my senior year in high school."
Gordon Korman

Montreal, Quebec, Canada

SPECIAL ANNIVERSARY EDITION!

tales of a
fourth grade
nothing

NEW YORK TIMES BESTSELLING AUTHOR

JUDY BLUME

Peter's got a big problem—
his little brother!

JOHN D. FITZGERALD

Illustrated by Mercer Mayer

More Adventures of the Great Brain

## ! fun fact

Growing up, Gordon's favorite books were the Great Brain series by John D. Fitzgerald. He also liked *Tales of a Fourth Grade Nothing* by Judy Blume.

In school, Gordon did well in his math and science classes. He also enjoyed reading.

Gordon also liked to write. He enjoyed creating funny sentences with his weekly spelling words. In seventh grade, Gordon's English teacher gave his class a big writing project. Students wrote whatever they wanted every day for four months.

Gordon used his creativity to write about two friends named Boots and Bruno. Gordon's friends loved the story!

"Although laughter may not solve anything, it sure makes the bad stuff a lot easier to take."
Gordon Korman

Gordon at age 22

When Gordon finished his story, he sent the **draft** to a **publisher** called Scholastic. They accepted it! Two years after it was written, *This Can't Be Happening at Macdonald Hall!* was **published**.

"Whatever an adult can do, somewhere in the world there's one 16-year-old who can do it as well."
Gordon Korman

! **fun fact**

Gordon's mom typed his first book for him.

Gordon continued writing throughout high school. He worked on his stories during summer vacations. By graduation, he had published several more books!

# A Writing Mastermind

New York University

**fun fact**

It usually takes Gordon around six months to write a book.

After high school, Gordon knew he wanted to be a writer. He went to college at New York University. He studied writing and film.

Gordon graduated from college in 1985. By that time, he had written even more books for children. Now he was ready to be a full-time writer!

"I love my job. The way I see it, I get paid for making things up – something I used to do for free."

Gordon Korman

Gordon worked on many books after finishing school. He usually wrote at least one per year!

Over the years, his books have won many awards. They have been printed in more than 30 different languages. These stories are still favorites of many readers today.

# Going on Adventures

Many of Gordon's books are funny. He writes the stories that he wanted to read as a kid. Readers are drawn in by the silly humor.

Gordon's characters often have **bold** personalities. They **rebel** against boring teachers. They also go on crazy adventures.

## SELECTED WORKS

**Macdonald Hall series (1978-1995)**

*The Twinkie Squad* (1992)

**The Monday Night Football Club series (1997-1998)**

*The Sixth Grade Nickname Game* (1998)

*No More Dead Dogs* (2002)

*Son of the Mob* (2002)

*Schooled* (2007)

**Swindle series (2008-)**

**Titanic series (2011)**

*Ungifted* (2012)

**Hypnotists series (2013-)**

**Masterminds series (2015-)**

Gordon also writes serious action stories. His Island, Everest, and Dive **trilogies** take readers on dangerous journeys. In these books, Gordon uses **suspense** to keep readers turning pages.

## fun fact

Gordon is one of the writers of the 39 Clues series. Rick Riordan and Linda Sue Park are other authors working on the project.

> "I try to make my characters funny and/or exciting because writing a novel is almost like living with those characters for a few months."
>
> Gordon Korman

## POP CULTURE CONNECTION

In 2013, the Swindle series came to life as a television movie on the Nickelodeon channel. Stars such as Jennette McCurdy, Noah Crawford, and Ariana Grande teamed up for the film.

Gordon's characters work together in these stories. Friendship and teamwork help them survive!

# Still Busy Writing

After many years of writing, Gordon continues to entertain readers. Today, he spends much of his time visiting schools and libraries.

"I always start off with something real, but then I unleash my imagination to make it more exciting, funnier, or a better story."
Gordon Korman

# IMPORTANT DATES

**1963:** Gordon Korman is born on October 23.

**1978:** Gordon's first book, *This Can't Be Happening at Macdonald Hall!*, is published.

**1981:** Gordon wins Canadian Authors' Association Air Canada Award for Most Promising Writer Under 35.

**1986:** *I Want to Go Home!* is presented with an International Reading Association Children's Choice Award.

**1987:** Gordon receives the Markham Civic Award for Cultural Achievement.

**1988:** The American Library Association lists *A Semester in the Life of a Garbage Bag* as an Editor's Choice.

**1992:** The Manitoba Young Readers' Choice Award is given to *The Zucchini Warriors*.

**1996:** Gordon marries his wife, Michelle.

**2016:** *Masterminds* wins the Silver Birch Award from the Ontario Library Association.

Gordon also writes regularly. He usually works on three books at a time. Whether it is a stand-alone novel or part of a series, Gordon continues to excite readers with new stories!

# Glossary

**bold**—brave and willing to take risks

**draft**—a version of something made before the final version

**novels**—longer written stories, usually about made-up characters and events

**published**—printed for a public audience

**publisher**—a company that makes and prints books

**rebel**—to act out against authority

**series**—a number of things that are connected in a certain order

**suspense**—a feeling of excitement or uncertainty

**trilogies**—series made up of three books

# To Learn More

## AT THE LIBRARY

Korman, Gordon. *This Can't Be Happening At Macdonald Hall!*. Richmond Hill, Ont.: Scholastic-TAB Publications, 1978.

Leaf, Christina. *Rick Riordan*. Minneapolis, Minn.: Bellwether Media, 2016.

Matthews, Sheelagh. *Gordon Korman*. New York, N.Y.: AV2 by Weigl, 2013.

## ON THE WEB

Learning more about Gordon Korman is as easy as 1, 2, 3.

1. Go to www.factsurfer.com.

2. Enter "Gordon Korman" into the search box.

3. Click the "Surf" button and you will see a list of related web sites.

With factsurfer.com, finding more information is just a click away.

# Index